Why Does Lightning Flash?

and other startling facts about electricity

By Angela Royston

Contents

Amazing electricity

Astounding power!

What has been around since long before the dinosaurs? What can kill you in an instant but also powers the fastest train in the world? It's truly shocking ... it's electricity!

So what is electricity?

Electricity is a form of energy. Energy is found in everything we do. Heat, light, sound and electricity are all different forms of energy. Nothing can happen without energy! Energy can change from one form into another. For example, electricity can be changed into light, heat and sound. Electrical energy scared and mystified people for thousands of years. This book will reveal its amazing secrets so read on!

At night, the city of Hong Kong is lit by brig lights and lasers — all thanks to electricity.

Name: **Thomas Alva Edison**

Dates: 1847–1931

Job: **The most famous inventor ever!**

Edison invented more than 1,000 different electrical gadgets. How's that for energy? His inventions included a light bulb and a moving picture camera. Was he good at school? No way! His teacher said he was 'addled', meaning she thought he couldn't think straight.

Strange...

Edison had so many bright ideas, he opened an 'inventions factory' at Menlo Park in New Jersey, USA. Here he employed hundreds of scientists and became known as the 'Wizard of Menlo'.

...but true

Thomas Alva Edison busy in his inventions factory

Scary lightning

What is it?

You don't want to tangle with lightning. A flash of lightning is a huge electrical **spark** that rips through the air at a fantastic speed – up to 140,000 kilometres per second! How's that for astonishing energy?

Sizzling heat

Some of the electrical energy in lightning changes into heat. The air around the flash is three times hotter than the Sun! Lightning strikes the highest or nearest object. Make sure it's not you because the intense heat could frazzle you to a crisp.

In the most powerful storms, several flashes of lightning can strike at the same time.

When you *see* lightning, count the seconds between the flash and the thunder: the shorter the gap, the closer the lightning. If the gap is less than 30 seconds, take shelter – but not under a tree!

Shocking experiment – DON'T try this!

Benjamin Franklin was sure that lightning was electricity. In 1752 he carried out an experiment which proved it.

Secret Diary of Benjamin Franklin's son, William

Date: June, 1752

Father is totally crazy! Today I helped him do a truly dangerous experiment. We sent a special kite up into a thundercloud. He tied a metal key to the kite string and waited. When he touched the key, he got a small electric shock. This proved that thunderclouds make electricity! He was so happy! And so was I – if lightning had struck the kite, he'd be dead now!

An experiment like Franklin's is very dangerous.

All in a flash

Why does lightning flash?

A thundercloud is full of energy. Tiny droplets of water and tiny pieces of ice are thrown around inside it and crash together. Think of dodgem cars inside a washing machine! What's the result of all that violence? Tiny **electrical particles** – called **static electricity** – spin off. Some electrical particles have a negative charge and the rest have a positive charge.

What on earth does that mean?

A charge is an amount of electrical energy. The particles with a positive charge collect at the top of the cloud and those with a negative charge collect at the bottom. You might think positives and negatives don't agree but you'd be wrong! They can't wait to get together. The positives rush towards the negatives causing lightning flashes.

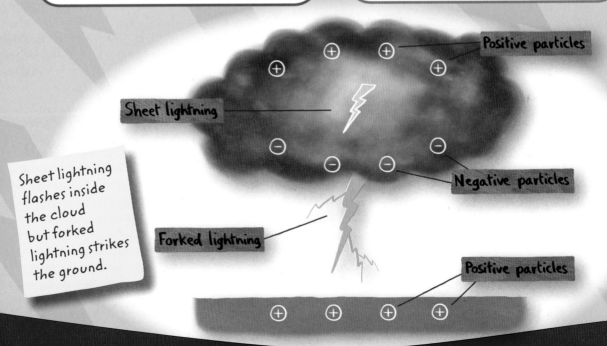

Positive particles

Sheet lightning

Negative particles

Sheet lightning flashes inside the cloud but forked lightning strikes the ground.

Forked lightning

Positive particles

Danger! Danger!

Forked lightning aims for the nearest, highest thing on the ground below. This can be a tall building or a tree. Sometimes it may be a person.* Eeeeek! What happens when lightning strikes an object?

LUCKY MISS!

Fred Brown is a keen golfer. He was too keen, because he carried on playing during a thunderstorm. Fred sheltered under a tree but it was struck by lightning. The tree exploded and caught fire! 'I can't believe I wasn't killed,' said Fred.

This massive tree was split in half by a mighty bolt of lightning.

*Want to read more about electric shocks? Go to page 18.

Hair-raising!

Ecstatic examples!

Lightning is an awesome and dangerous example of static electricity, but static electricity crops up in the most extraordinary places.

Stroking the cat

Have you ever noticed that when you stroke your cat, you sometimes get a small shock, like an insect sting? This happens because static electricity builds up in your pet's fur.

Static electricity can make a cat's skin tingle, even before you get a shock.

Hair-raising

When you comb your hair, look in the mirror. Are some of the hairs beginning to stand on end? That's static electricity for you!

Try this!

Want to move a can without touching or blowing it? Easy – use static electricity.

What you need:

- a balloon
- your hair
- a dry, empty aluminium drinks can

What to do:

1 Blow up the balloon and knot the end.

2 Put the can on its side on a smooth surface.

3 Rub the balloon against your hair for ten seconds. This charges the balloon with static electricity.

4 Quickly put the balloon near, but not touching, the can. The can should roll towards it.

5 Move the balloon away slowly. Does the can follow?

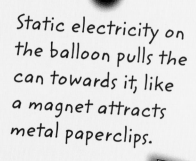

Static electricity on the balloon pulls the can towards it, like a magnet attracts metal paperclips.

Going with the flow

Long-lasting electricity

Static electricity lasts only an instant, so it's no good for lighting your home! Luckily, scientists discovered how to make their own electricity. The big break-through was made by Michael Faraday in 1831. He couldn't wait to tell his friend Humphrey Davy.

29 October 1831

Dear Humph,

Today I produced a steady current of electricity! I used a huge magnet and a spinning disc to make the electricity. Never mind the details – let's just call it a dynamo. The current flowed in a circuit from the dynamo along wires back to the dynamo. Take a look at my sketch to see what I mean.

Your friend,
Michael

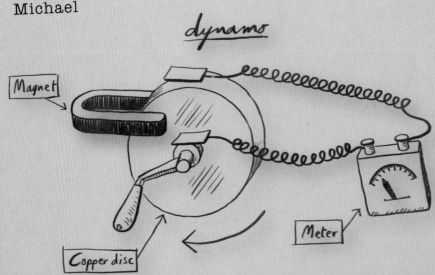

dynamo

Magnet

Meter

Copper disc

Electrical lingo

Mr Faraday used a lot of strange words in his letter. What do they mean?

Dynamo	A machine that makes electricity. It's also called a generator.
Current	A flow of electricity.
Circuit	A circuit is like a race track for electricity. Instead of a circle of road, an electrical circuit is a pathway for electric current to flow around. An electrical circuit also needs a supply of electricity and something to show that the electricity is flowing*.

So you thought a current was something to eat? It sounds the same but check the spelling: currant buns, not current buns!

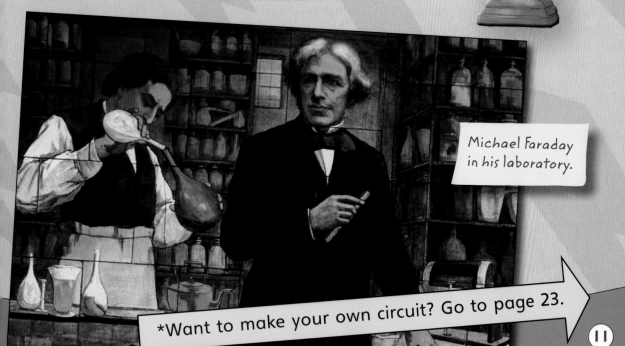

Michael Faraday in his laboratory.

*Want to make your own circuit? Go to page 23.

Lights on!

Inventors get busy

Once scientists had electric currents and circuits, they started inventing all sorts of electrical machines and gadgets, including a telephone and a toaster. However, Edison's big invention was a whole system of electric lighting that could be used in homes.

Hard work

Inventing isn't just sitting around having bright ideas – it's hard work! Edison wanted a cheap light bulb that would shine for many hours. Other inventors' light bulbs only lasted for a few hours. He needed a material that would become white hot but wouldn't burn when electricity passed through it. Hundreds of assistants tried everything, even crocodile skin and human hair! Which one worked best? A cotton thread!

THOMAS A. EDISON
ELECTRIC-LAMP
No. 223,898   Pat'd Jan. 27, 1880

Don't forget my other inventions. They included a phonograph – a way of recording and playing back sound.

Edison's lightbulb was patented in 1880. This meant that no one else could claim the idea was theirs.

Look at that!

A light bulb is no use on its own. It needs wires, switches, **sockets** and more to make it shine. Edison invented the lot! In 1882 he invited reporters, scientists and other bigwigs to Pearl Street, New York. Why? Read on ...

AMAZING SPECTACLE!

Last night Mr Edison switched on electric lights in the rooms of 25 buildings in Pearl Street, New York. A crowd of important people were invited to watch. When the generators were switched on, they screeched and groaned, and sparks flashed everywhere! People fled in terror! Slowly the lights began to glow red.

Everyone cheered when the lights all shone brightly!

Edison's Dynamo Room in Pearl Street, New York, was the world's first electric **power station.**

Lights out!

Plug in and switch on

Today we have hundreds of electrical machines and gadgets. Count the electrical **appliances** in your kitchen – don't forget the fridge and the microwave oven. Every room uses electricity. Some people even have an electric toothbrush.

Power cut!

You probably take electrical machines and gadgets for granted, but suppose the electricity stopped flowing and there is a power cut. It can happen! Imagine it – no computer games, no television and no electric lights!

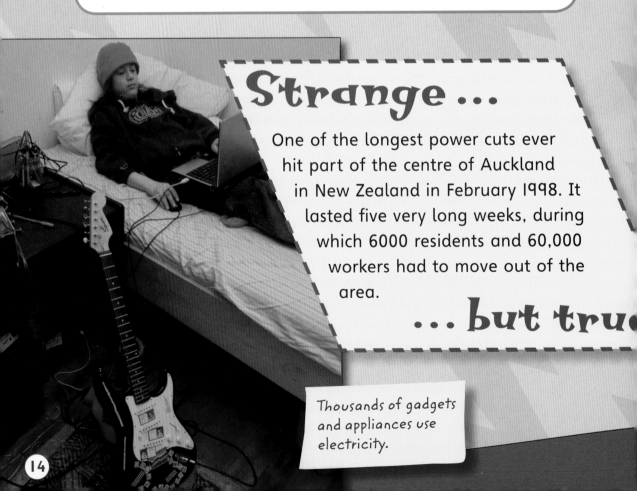

Strange...

One of the longest power cuts ever hit part of the centre of Auckland in New Zealand in February 1998. It lasted five very long weeks, during which 6000 residents and 60,000 workers had to move out of the area.

... but tru

Thousands of gadgets and appliances use electricity.

Blackout!

In 2003, 55 million people in North-Eastern United States and Canada suddenly found themselves without electricity. It was one of the biggest power cuts ever.

On 14 August 2003 the whole of New York and beyond was in darkness.

My Diary by Maria, New York, USA

Date: 14 August 2003

All of New York is in darkness, and also everywhere from here to Michigan. Just heard that Ontario's out too! Mom couldn't get home by train (it's electric!), so she had to walk. Weird having no electricity, no computer or TV, but it's kind of exciting too. Everyone is out on their steps talking to each other. That's a first!

High powered

Follow the current

Where does the electricity for your electrical gadgets come from? It comes from the socket in the wall but how does it get there? The answer is through the **national grid** from power stations.

Electrifying or what?

Electric **cables** run under pavements and streets – you walk over them every day! They are part of thousands of different circuits that join together to make the national grid. Power stations produce electricity and feed it into the grid.

Huge electric pylons carry the electric cables that bring electricity from power stations to your home.

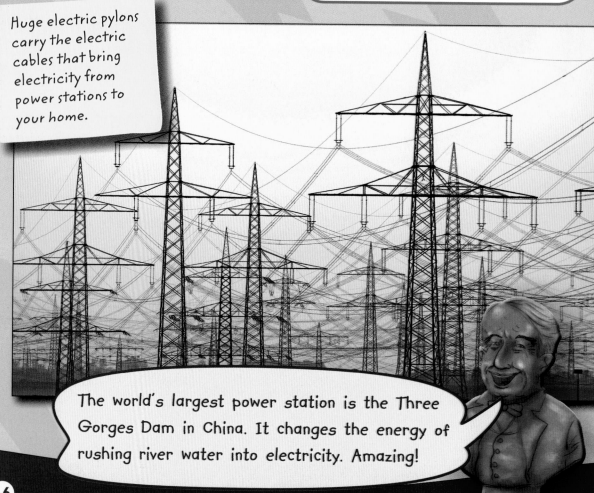

The world's largest power station is the Three Gorges Dam in China. It changes the energy of rushing river water into electricity. Amazing!

Super powerful

The electricity that leaves the power stations is super charged with energy. It is 100 times stronger that the electricity that comes into your home!

Viva la voltage!

Voltage measures electrical energy: a higher voltage means more energy. The electricity leaving a power station needs massive energy to travel all through the grid. However, if you used high voltage energy at home, your TV and everything else would explode! The grid includes **transformers**. These brilliant devices change the voltage from 22,000 volts down to about 220 volts. Your TV is safe – phew!

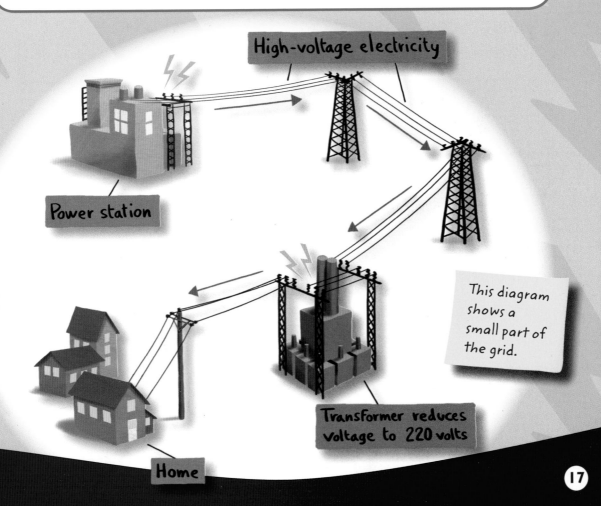

High-voltage electricity

Power station

This diagram shows a small part of the grid.

Transformer reduces voltage to 220 volts

Home

The shocking truth

Deadly dangerous

Electricity is dangerous! The higher the voltage, the more deadly it is, but even the electricity that comes into your home and school is strong enough to seriously harm you.

The grisly effect

When electricity passes through you to the ground, you get an electric shock. Some of the electricity changes into ferocious heat, which can cause burns. An electric shock can stop the heart beating and make the muscles 'freeze'. This can mean that the person getting the electric shock can't let go of whatever is causing it! Aaaagh!

Strange...

Birds can sit on electric wires without getting a shock. This is because electricity travels from something high voltage to something low voltage, such as the post. The birds are fine because they are not touching the wire and the post at the same time!

...but true

WHAT TO DO IF SOMEBODY GETS AN
ELECTRIC SHOCK

SHOCK TREATMENT

1 *Make sure the person is not touching the cause of the shock.*

2 *If they are, switch off the electricity safely – at the plug or at the electricity meter.*

3 *Phone for a doctor or ambulance.*

Stay safe

Don't take risks with electricity – it's too shocking! Don't play with electric sockets or push things into them. You don't want 220 volts striking your fingers! Don't touch bare wires or use gadgets that have bare wires.

Strange ...

Electric eels make enough electricity to harm a human. Don't swim in the River Amazon in South America because that's where they live.

... but true

This sign warns you that there is dangerous electricity nearby.

Batteries are best

Battery power

What do a watch and a remote control have in common? They both have batteries. The batteries make electricity.

This mobile phone uses batteries.

No shock

Batteries are so small you can easily carry them around (unlike a power station!). They make a small amount of electricity – usually just a few volts. That's enough to power small gadgets but not enough to give you a shock.

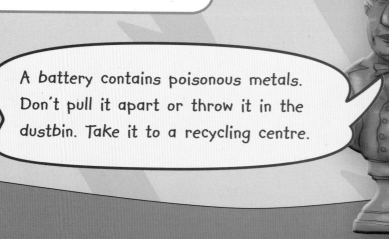

A battery contains poisonous metals. Don't pull it apart or throw it in the dustbin. Take it to a recycling centre.

How does it work?

A battery works a bit like a thundercloud – a small, controlled thundercloud! When the battery is being used, chemicals inside it make negative and positive particles. Every battery has a positive end, called a positive **terminal**, and a negative terminal. Electricity flows from the positive terminal, through the gadget and back to the negative terminal.

Strange...

In 1800, Alessandro Volta made the first battery. He got the idea after he put a silver coin on his tongue and a coin made of a different metal next to it. The metals generated electricity, which made his tongue tingle. DON'T try it!

...but true

Volta's battery (which he called a 'Voltaic pile' after himself) was made of metals, cardboard and salt water.

Circuit wizardry

Electric magic

Electricity can seem like magic – sometimes it flows, sometimes it doesn't. Experiment with a simple circuit, and you'll soon see how it works.

What you need to make a simple circuit

1. A battery to supply the electricity.
2. A light bulb or buzzer that works when an electric current passes through it.
3. Electric wires to connect the battery to the appliance and the appliance to the battery.

Keep it flowing

A circuit* has no end or beginning, so the current keeps flowing – but only if the circuit has no gaps or breaks.

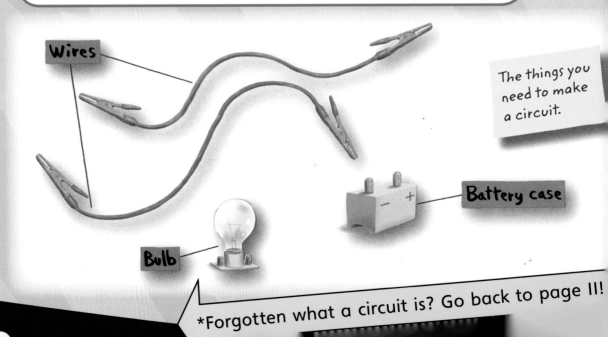

Wires

The things you need to make a circuit.

Battery case

Bulb

*Forgotten what a circuit is? Go back to page 11!

Try this!

Got the things you need to make a circuit? OK –
it's time to explore electric currents.

What you need:

- two batteries

- four pieces of electric wire

- two torch bulbs

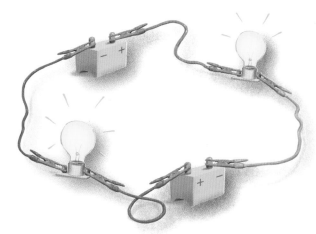

What to do:

1 Make a simple circuit using one battery, two wires and a
torch bulb. Does the bulb light up? No? Make sure you have
connected the positive terminal of the battery to the positive
terminal of the bulb.

2 Use another wire to connect the second torch bulb. Is the
light brighter or dimmer now?

3 Use the last wire to connect
the second battery.
What happens to the lights?

4 Change the circuit to get a
brighter light.

5 At each step, check your
results with the answers
in the post-it note.

Step 2: Adding another bulb
in the circuit makes the light
from both bulbs dimmer.
Step 3: The lights should
become brighter.
Step 4: Two batteries and
one torch bulb will
give the brightest light.

Current conductors

Carrying the current

What's an electrical conductor? Is it like the conductor of an orchestra? Does it wave a stick and tell the light bulb when to shine? No! Electricity is a bit lazy. It likes easy things to flow along and that is exactly what an electrical conductor is. It allows electricity to flow easily. No circuit is complete without them, but not all conductors are part of a circuit.

Lightning protector

A lightning conductor is fixed to the top of a high building or other objects that might be damaged by lightning. When lightning hits the rod of a conductor the powerful electricity flows down a cable and safely into the ground. Cool!

Shockingly wet

Water and electricity are very dangerous together because water is a good conductor. Watch out: mixing electricity and water will give you a shock! Stay safe and NEVER use electrical gadgets when you are wet. NEVER touch electric sockets or light switches with wet hands!

Strange...

Electric rays stun their prey with a bolt of electricity! They don't even have to touch the other fish – the seawater conducts the electricity to them!

... but true

An electric ray waits for 'dinner' to swim by and then zaps it!

Does it buzz?

Find out which materials make the best conductors.

What you need:

- a battery
- a buzzer
- three electrical wires

- objects to test, e.g. a metal spoon, a piece of string, aluminium foil, cotton thread, a coin

What to do:

1 Make a circuit with the battery, the buzzer and the three wires. Leave a gap between two of the wires.

2 Attach a wire to each end of the spoon to close the gap between the wires. Does the buzzer buzz?

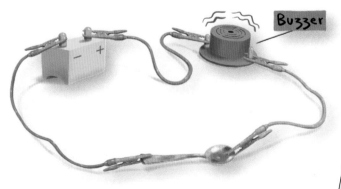

Buzzer

3 Test each object. Which objects make the buzzer buzz?

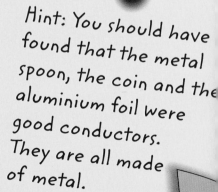

Hint: You should have found that the metal spoon, the coin and the aluminium foil were good conductors. They are all made of metal.

Bad conductors

Electricity can't flow easily through a bad conductor. You might think that bad conductors are useless, but they can also be good. Steam irons and toasters are just two gadgets that wouldn't work without them.

Making toast

The metal mesh inside a toaster is a bad conductor. As the current tries to find a way through, some of the electrical energy is changed into heat. The metal mesh is now red-hot! Up pops the toast! Delicious – pass the jam!

Shock protectors

No flow

Some materials don't conduct electricity at all. They are called insulators and they are definitely not useful in a circuit. However, insulators are brilliant! They protect you from electric shocks.

SHOES SAVE BOY'S LIFE!

Harley Sutton-Dormer got an electric shock when he switched on a faulty hairdryer. "A bright blue bolt of electricity went right down his arm," said his mother. "His shoes were made of plastic and foam." The ambulance man said his plastic shoes stopped the flow of electricity. This stopped the shock going through his legs to the ground. The shoes probably saved his life.

Electric wires are inside a plastic covering. The plastic insulates you from the electricity flowing inside. That's why you don't get a shock from the wires of your electrical appliances or gadgets.

Try this!

Want to protect yourself from electric eels*?
Design a fantastic swimming suit using the
test below.

What you need:

- a battery
- a light bulb
- three electrical wires
- materials to test for the suit: a plastic bag, a piece of aluminium foil, a rubber band, a sheet of paper, and anything else you can think of!

What to do:

1 Set up a simple circuit. Leave a gap between two of the wires.

2 Test each of the materials and sort them into insulators and conductors.

3 Which material would insulate you from the eel and make the best diving suit? Think about what would happen to the material when it is wet. Now design your suit.

*Forgotten about electric eels? Go back to page 19!

An electrifying future

Bright future

Do you want to know what the future will be like? Look at the things people are inventing now. Today's crazy ideas are tomorrow's 'must haves', and many involve electricity!

Fantastic fuel cell

A fuel cell is a bit like a battery. It uses a chemical reaction to combine the gas hydrogen with the gas oxygen to make water. At the same time, it makes electricity. Sound crazy? Maybe. Does it work? Yes! Fuel cells are already used in some cars, buses and trains.

Strange...

Hydrogen and oxygen are both gases at normal temperature but when they join together, they make water!

... but true

This bus has a hydrogen fuel cell but fuel cells are too expensive for us all to have them yet.

Powered by hydrogen fuel cell – zero emission bus

BALLARD First

Another red bus
going green for LONDON

hydrogen
bus

Micro power

Tiny fuel cells can take the place of batteries in mobile phones, cameras and other gadgets. Mobile phones already exist that break down cola and soil to get hydrogen for the micro fuel cell. How weird is that? Some micro cells run on water. Electricity splits the water into hydrogen and oxygen. Then the fuel cell recombines them to make electricity.

Wow! I wish I was alive now. My brain is crackling with ideas for new inventions!

Glossary

appliances household machines, such as washing machines and freezers

cables several wires twisted together to make a thick bundle of wires

electrical particles extremely tiny parts which have an electrical charge

electricity meter simple machine which measures how much electricity is used.

national grid network that supplies the whole country with electricity

power station building where electricity is produced

sockets places where you connect electric plugs to get electricity

spark flash of light produced when electricity jumps from one place to another

static electricity electricity that is produced by rubbing different materials against each other

terminal place where electricity leaves or enters a battery

transformers gadgets that change the voltage of an electric current

Index